Pasadena Rose Poets Poetry Collection 2022

Not So Perfect Storm

Edited by
Gerda Govine Ituarte

Pasadena Rose Poets Poetry Collection 2022
Not So Perfect Storm

Copyright © 2022 by Gerda Govine Ituarte

All rights reserved. No part of this book may be reproduced or transmitted in any form or by any means without written permission of the author.

ISBN 9781737711346

Library of Congress Control Number: 2022940748

Cover Art by Luis Ituarte
Cover design by Teresa Mei Chuc

Published by Shabda Press
Duarte, California
www.shabdapress.com

PROLOGUE

Our first publication, *Pasadena Rose Poets Poetry Collection 2019 Reflection. Resistance. Reckoning. Resurrection.* was published in September prior to COVID-19 initial invasion. To celebrate our 6th Anniversary, July 2022, we decided to launch our second book, *Pasadena Rose Poets Poetry Collection 2022 Not So Perfect Storm.* This journey was shaped by unchartered terrain which caused us to keep adjusting and reinventing, laced with a litany of surprising challenges, chaos, and change. Not only in our communities, but all over the world. Illness and death snatched family and friends, economic hardships hunkered down; ravaging wildfires multiplied; January 6th riot erupted; murder of George Floyd and rare guilty verdict, protests mushroomed; appointment of Justice Ketanji Brown to the US Supreme Court; and the continuing war of genocide in Ukraine.

We continued to read, write, publish, create, and stay connected with each other and our communities while exploring and observing new experiences within reach woven with threads of randomness. A bird flies so close you feel the warm air from wings enter your ear; walking stop, look down, a shiny dime glistens at your feet, and encounter a bear in your dreams as hint of danger dissolves when you say No! No! the bear walks away.

Creating, and delivering poetry in unexpected places is our norm. We keep opening and entering spaces that allows us to breathe, see, think, feel, as words flow on to the page. How can our children, grandchildren, and future generations know what it is was like to live and walk with the wind instead of in the wind. We hunkered down and wrote because we can't help it. We do not fold, instead expand, and keep going. Our survival leans in as we look into a translucent future from this *Not So Perfect Storm.* Our saving grace is the urge and need to write, to document what we see, and feel since our work mirrors life real or imagined. The first gift of the day is the fact that we woke up.

ACKNOWLEDGEMENT

The Pasadena Rose Poets, Teresa Mei Chuc, Damian, Kate Gale, Hazel Clayton Harrison, Gerda Govine Ituarte, Shahé Mankerian, Toni Mosley, Carla Sameth and Annette Wong continue to create insightful work that calls forth wonder, humanity, humor, and authenticity. They weave their words into tapestries of life as we traverse unexpected places and spaces. Thank you to Teresa Mei Chuc Publisher, Shabda Press. This is her first publishing project since the *Altadena Library Review 2020*. Teresa stated, "I am excited, and this is a good way to emerge from the Pandemic." Continuing kudos to Christine Reeder, Senior Librarian, Adult Services, Pasadena Central Library; Bocajapa Writing Group, Manuela Gomez, Kerri Kumasaka, Carla Sameth; and Carrizozo Artist Residency, Carrizozo, New Mexico. Kudos to Luis Ituarte, Contributing Artist, and Photographer Alfred Haymond.

PASADENA ROSE POETS STATEMENT

Teresa Mei Chuc

Maple Leaf – My First Encounter With Poetry
I was a child walking home from elementary school. In the fall, the leaves would drift to the ground so on my way home, I would see dry maple leaves on the sidewalk. I was enchanted by their beauty and would pick them up, hold them in my hand. I remember writing one of my very first poems about it. My observation of the maple leaf. Five points, the crown of a king, veins like rivers flowing through jungles. The leaf encompassed these grand things but at the same time it was so fragile, it could crunch and crumble at the slight movement of my fingers. I think this was when I realized what a metaphor was. I was that leaf. It was moments like this that made me connect with poetry. I could communicate so much meaning about my life through an autumn leaf.

Damian
I don't find it easy to refer to myself as a poet because I don't know when I started writing poetry. I do know that if I don't sieve my experiences and try to distill them down with the words that form in my head, I may very well die. So, I keep speaking, I keep writing, I keep witnessing. Senses alert. Ready to share. I'm a plagiarist of experience; sometimes I exploit my own, sometimes I leverage the experiences of others. Some days I think of myself as a journalist, some days a translator. I am a comedian, a cynic, an advocate. At my most unkind, I've been an informant, and betrayer of secrets. I don't always know why I create but I am insatiably curious, always hungry for life, and words–spoken or written–just help me from bursting at the seams.

Dr. Kate Gale
I write poetry because without poetry I cannot think my way out of the well in which I find myself too often. Neither of my parents wanted me and growing up, poetry became my thing. I didn't learn how to write it until graduate

school, and the joy of it is that I am still learning and always will be and even when I'm off exploring the universe, poetry is ready for me to come back into the clearing in the wood.

Hazel Clayton Harrison
Both of my parents were storytellers. Some of my earliest memories are of them sitting on the edge of my bed at night reciting poems or telling me stories. In grade school I became an avid reader. I loved to read nursery rhymes and spent hours in the school library reading Grimm's and Hans Christian Anderson fairy tales. At first it was the sound of words that captivated me. The whiz, bang, boom, snap, crackle, pop of words. And as I learned their meanings, I began to pen my own poems. When I received praises from my parents and teachers for my rudimentary writings, I knew I was destined to become a writer. My enslaved ancestors were musicians, poets, and storytellers. Because they were forbidden by law to read or write, they handed down their poetry, songs, and stories by word of mouth. Now I feel a responsibility to write them down. Perhaps I write because poetry and storytelling are in my DNA. I write to create worlds I can explore and inhabit. I write to know what I think, what I like and dislike, who I am. I write to make sense of a world that often makes no sense. I write because writing is therapy and helps me to heal my broken wings.

Dr. Gerda Govine Ituarte
I began writing poetry to ease the sorrow and grief due to my youngest adult daughter's illness and death within a nine-month period. Every morning I would sit on the balcony of La Casa del Túnel: Art Center as birds flew back and forth over the man-made border in Tijuana, B.C., Mexico. Words erupted on to the page as I "let myself out," with the power to breathe easier—to pause, think, feel, and inhale the gift of freedom. I write because I can't help it. I trust, honor and love words that reciprocate. We all live in a world that is raining words. As a poet my grounding comes from being able to walk between the raindrops with wonder, inspiration, adventure, and peace. To keep the words alive and offer poetry to touch and impact others.

Shahé Mankerian
I started writing poetry as a teenager. Being a Lebanese-Armenian immigrant, I muted myself in the public schools of Pasadena. I lacked the confidence and vocabulary to speak. The English language sounded so superfluid; in contrast, I had erected an inner dam to hide my insecurities and the incoherent articulation of feelings and thoughts.

By 11th grade, I stumbled upon Mrs. Reyna's Creative Writing class at Pasadena High School who made poetry accessible and stigma-free. I fell in love with its short form, compact sentences, erratic punctuation, and line breaks that resembled teenage heartbreaks. I was hooked. All the suppressed speech suddenly became liberated. Poetry blanketed my thick, Armenian accent. I didn't need to stutter to find my next phrase. Words on paper didn't suffer from inferiority complexes. I could finally confess my love to the girl sitting in front of me in biology class without hiccups, without sounding broken or incomprehensible. Forty years later, I stand guilty of having a love affair with words. I write poetry because it creates bridges with my youth, with familial ghosts, with the cinema of unrest, with a caravan of distant trauma. It gives me time to play with my subconscious. Why do I write? Because Bukowski said, a poet must write because "being still would / drive you to madness or / suicide or murder… / if you have been chosen, / it will do it by / itself and it will keep on doing it / until you die or it dies in you. / There is no other way."

Toni Mosley
My Dad would say there is nothing worse than a dumb pretty woman. When I came home, he encouraged me to write a story each day about what happened at school. With the proviso, *I know you will always be pretty, but I do not want you to be dumb.* Working as an administrator in the non-profit sector with children one of their assignments was to write stories about what happened at school each day. This resurrected the call of my heart and intuition to begin writing and flung open wide the author/poet/storyteller trying to get out. I focus on writing poetry and completed my draft memoir, "Dead Flies on the Window Sill." My amazing journey continues.

Carla Sameth

I wrote poetry throughout my life but in smaller doses, every so often as opposed to other genres. I wrote more frequently in (memoir, nonfiction, fiction). When I got my MFA, I began to experiment more with poetry and study with some poets. Gerda Govine Ituarte, founder of the Pasadena Rose Poets, identified me as a poet, selected me to be one of the Pasadena Rose Poets, and from there I found myself increasingly drawn to poetry and other shorter/hybrid forms. As I got older, the world changed, we entered the pandemic I found myself drawn almost exclusively to poems and hybrid or flash/short form whether fiction or nonfiction. Something about the sense of urgency encapsulated in an economy of words. My outlook as a writer is framed by my identity as a 63-year-old queer Jewish woman, a mother and a mother of a Black son, and wife of a trans man. And all the vulnerability, joy and strength that is part of that identity. I write for connection and to offer a sense of resilience and possibility to those who relate to issues I write about. As a writer, I hope to help readers feel less alone. As a teacher, I strive to help others tell their stories and hone their craft while experimenting with new forms. The journey of motherhood informs much of my writing. Finally, I write to process, reflect, and digest what happens to me and in the world.

Annette Wong

We all tell ourselves stories about who we are. Our narratives inform how we move about the world. They shape the arcs of our lives. As a writer, I am attuned to the nuances of language. How we use language signals how we feel on a conscious and subconscious level by listening deeply and attentively.

Teresa Mei Chuc

Chinese Female Kung-Fu Superheroes

are real. They jump from roof-top
to roof-top, do a backward flip
down to the concrete floor and land
perfectly on two feet.

The metal of swords clang,
the body moves with the precision
of a praying mantis striking
its prey.

Their dresses are colorful, long
and lacy, billow and flair
with each turn and twist.

Jewelry in the hair dangles and sparkles.

Chinese female kung-fu superheroes
are smart, fight bad guys, do good deeds,
and risk their lives.
They appear when least expected.

Chinese female kung-fu superheroes
never give up. They travel often alone
by foot through mountains. They work hard
training to master various martial arts forms.

They do not care about Barbies,
those plastic dolls of only one hair color
that just looked pretty in the 80's. They aren't
impressed; they do not want a boring life.

Chinese female kung-fu superheroes venture out
and save cities against villains. They steal into the night
in their black ninja-like suits, soundlessly through a house
to recover a magical sword and to release a prisoner,
knowing exactly where to press with their two fingertips
to freeze the guards and to accomplish their mission.

Teresa Mei Chuc

After Jeannine Hall Gailey's Becoming the Villainess

The Unknown Woman

As she washes the grains of rice,
stirs the embers for fire
for the soup in the stone pot cooking,
she ponders words and sounds
and feelings.
She writes poems in the wind,
in the soil,
in the clouds.
The words sweep back
and forth with the bamboo
broom with grass bristles,
go up in plumes
with the chicken feathered duster.
As she carries the water from the river,
and washes the clothes,
the words swoosh, swoosh,
back and forth, back and forth.
In her mind, sway,
never really going anywhere.
At night, as she removes the intricate
flower-shaped pin from her hair,
all the poems tumble down.
As she closes her eyes
for the night, gathered
around her arms,
verses soft as her silk robe
pressed next to her quietly singing
heart.
Moonlight in the night,
a glow in her dark eyes
behind a curtain of skin.

Teresa Mei Chuc

Evolution: Danaus plexippus plexippus

a Monarch flickers its orange and black
lashes on a milkweed stem.
Tongue uncurling to drink the poisonous,
white sap.
Taking into its body the reason for its
survival – its ability to live with poison
and become it. It takes a bird once
to learn the lesson in eating a
Monarch.
How we survive, take our poisons and turn them
into milky white sap that sustains us.
Spread our patterned wings and be
harbinger – of flowers, plant, food, and
water.

Teresa Mei Chuc

Today

Today, someone died on Skid Row
and it will not be on the news

Someone was stabbed on Skid Row
and it will not be on the news

Someone was shot on Skid Row
and it will not be on the news

A mentally ill person was dropped off on Skid Row
and it will not be on the news

Someone was raped on Skid Row
and it will not be on the news

Someone was starving on Skid Row
and it will not be on the news

Someone was being trafficked on Skid Row
and it will not be on the news

Someone was high on meth on Skid Row
and it will not be on the news

The street was lined with disabled people on Skid Row
and it will not be on the news

Today, a child was homeless on Skid Row
and it will not be on the news

We let people die on Skid Row
and it will not be on the news

Teresa Mei Chuc

Tasting the Rain

Thích Nhất Hạnh says that when I eat an orange,
I could taste the clouds, the rain, the sunshine,
my late grandmother's love when she planted this tree
nearly half a century ago. Hear her voice conversing with leaves.
Feel the fluttering wings of bees covered in pollen
and see the iridescent hummingbird that visits daily drunk
on the nectar of orange blossoms.

Teresa Mei Chuc

Crying Makes You Feel Better

crying is okay like my 12th grade
student says he cries

the stress
balancing school,
work, family
during the covid-19 pandemic
nine hour work shifts
pushing heavy grocery carts
exhaustion

there are carts
left at the back
of the parking lot
where he needs
to walk that extra
few minutes
that extra amount
of energy left
squeezed out of him
to push the carts back
to the front of the store

Teresa Mei Chuc

Damian

Beyond the breakers

Standing on a pier at night, away from the shore, over the water, existing in two spaces.

In the dark, ocean and sky lay against each other but refuse to call themselves horizon.

The dock is built with scraps of jetsam, pieces of sadness, and can't be used for mooring.

Underneath, the tide rises or falls depending on the moon's mood or distance from Earth.

Dead-weight anchors drowning pillars that use their strength to keep the construct above water.

In the morning, the stars go back into hiding, and lovers always head back to the sand.

Damian

Expulsion from Eden

on nights while drinking down our divinity,
I watched your black-light heart glow violet against white cotton sheets.

Filled with as much whiskey as wonder,
we laid down to tell each other tales of lives unlived, dreams unfulfilled,
and we always parted ways with poetry too painful to take with us in
the morning.

In cars parked from view
you savor finite moments
because love comes fast

lust stretched on window
showing neighbors you were starved
but love don't live here

drunk under moon-shine
you fall and laugh at yourself
love like bed, broken

nature is not interested in morality and the dead do not carry the burden
of mistakes.

There are beautiful things in this world and there are sad things too,
and we can never be sure which there is more of, or prepare for which may
strike first.

Damian

Wildfire

Ash falls on a wooded labyrinth of twisted roots, stumps, and
scorched earth.
Willows once wept here
and the ruins used to resemble homes.

A wiry child unearthed a muse, in art, in music, in words
all because of a kiss on the cheek
that one unforgettable summer.

A ghost drifts aimlessly on dead land in search of love,
by way of time travel,
toward a past that is petrified.

Hues in the sky overhead once painted a story of joyful youth,
cheerful adolescence, an adulthood filled with contentment,
now the picture seems violent and unsettling.

This is the origin of your dreams and ambition
and it has been distilled down to abstraction.
Lament the injustice of nature,
the wind blows hot and howls a dirge just for you.

Damian

Bubble

A family of bubbles bloom from the tip of a cap atop a bottle of dishwashing detergent
squeezed while washing dishes.

An infinitesimal representation of the big bang—a miracle.
Have you ever witnessed a miracle before?

The beginning of a universe floats gently away and worries dissolve
as effervescent life spawns.

These newly formed worlds ride currents of breath, then disperse and become the cosmos.
For a moment you are God.

A law or formula could explain the way light refraction works, but it's not needed to enjoy the magenta, blue, green, yellow, and orange light cascading across each sphere.

Fragile soapy membranes cradle ambivalence, and sometimes the only thing separating a good day from a tragic one, is a smile.

Pop!

Damian

Published in Pasadena Rose Poets Poetry Collection 2019

THE DEAD & THE LIVING

violent
shadows
impressed
upon
our
graves
sharp
black
and
cold
cast
from
those
we
left
on
the
surface
angry & alone

Damian

Published in Altadena Poetry Review Anthology 2016

Warm Water

I was thirty when I met my father for the first time.
I shook his hand and said,
"I'm running late for a flight but maybe we can chat the next time we meet."
He replied,
"I'm sure we have a lot to talk about."
I saw him again four years later
in Miami.
Neither of us spoke much.
I remember him standing in the warm waters of south beach,
water to his knees, smiling,
and I tried to smile too
but he was just so ordinary.
I thought, it wasn't worth the energy
to smile for someone so average—
Must have been the same thought he had when I was a baby
Interesting,
genetics maybe…

Damian

Published in Pasadena Rose Poets Poetry Collection 2019

Kate Gale

In All the Movies

Men push back the women, take the horses.
Women rake leaves, fill pails of water, stack wood.
Men ride off, row shallow boats, sail big ships.
Women crowd the marketplace, buy ribbons.

When the men come to a new town, they demand food.
Drinks, beds, music, stories. The women provide all this.
The men take their stories to the next town and sell them.
Sleep with new women. Eat their food.

Men thrust feet into boots. Walk all over God's world.
Women corral their children, teach them to read.
Women plant roses and summer squash.
Men buy roses for other women.

We cry along the riverbank. Give us roses.
Give us stories and books, make us sing.
The men ride by, laugh, pause to see us wet.
Stooping to wash linens and catch fish.

We wave them on, Don't stop and stare, we say.
Your rage is air. Give us something we can taste.
Give us darkness between your legs, they say.
We're all darkness we say, we're nothing but darkness.

Kate Gale

Hanging

After crime,
punishment.

I was hanged.
Survived the hanging.

My neck has rope burn scars.
I will be hung again.

I should be punished.
I've heard since I was born.

As a kid, they'd say, You are going to be punished.
I'd say, Let's get it over with.

You fall.
Grace is where you fall from.

Earth is where you land.
Evil and fall the first story.

The only way out of fire is to fly.
The only way to fly is to grow wings.

Kate Gale

Medusa's Cookbook

Thin layers of pastry
like grasshopper's wings
salt
almond paste
nutmeg
cloves—an unopened flower bud
cinnamon—a spiraled brown quill
honey
crushed nuts

Kate Gale

Wound Care

Crossed to the other side of the street to avoid the wounded.
Gone to sleep to forget the wounded.

Watched the wounded on television,
Watched wounding on television.

Read fantastical stories of wounding.
Written fantastical stories of one's own wounding.

Hidden wounds up your sleeve, down your pants.
Through your body, under your socks, between your toes.

In the curve of arms and legs.
In the radius of the abdominal cavity.

Lasting wounds due to damage to underlying structures –
bone, muscle, tendon, arteries, nerves.

Cosmetic results not the primary consideration for wound repair.
Bites cause high rate of infection. Animal bites. Human bites.

We did not mean to wound others, but we did.
We wounded our friends. We wounded our lovers.

On my husband's back is a salt heart. I swim
every day in the ocean, ride behind him on the motorcycle

the salt heart where my breasts press against his shirt.
His heart has a new valve.

One long dark scar cross his chest.
A wound of slicing deeply.

Forcing back the rib cage, taking out his heart,
replacing valve in the heart chamber with titanium.

He ticks like a clock. When I say,
I have been wounded; I mean darkness.

Cherry blossoms open for fourteen days.
Petals drop. Leaves begin.

Be there for the first opening of white on pink.
Be there when the white on pink is blinding.

Be there when petals drop and green arrives.
Be there into the green and falling of leaves.

The bark sings to you. The leaves sing;
the cherry blossoms sing. Of wounding.

Of healing. Of white on pink. Of blossoms.
Feel petals blowing toward you. Feel morning come.

Kate Gale

Snakes In My Hair

I wish I weren't so fat.
Beauty would shield me.

I wish I made more money.
I'd have walls and greenery.

I want to be the center of someone's universe
The cave is cold.

I want someone to lick me.
The walls are wet and slimy.

There is no burble in the wood.
I'm hungry but dare not eat.

All the men in the world are eating pizza, nachos, cheese sandwiches.
All the women in the world are eating celery, radishes, lettuce.

I want a man to make my heart wild.
Like windows in a Japan, spring, pink and white petals of morning.

This morning.
I exited the cave.

Found a machete.
Severed the snakes.

Washed my body.
Anointed my head with oil.

Sure my cups run over.
Don't put your hands around my waist.

Don't even try.
Cup my breasts. I dare you.

I smell of sweetness.
I eat thickets of blackberries all afternoon.

Have you ever wished to be transformed?
This is that story.

You can walk out of the cave into the bright sunlight.
The curse is a story.
The flowering tree is a story.
The wings are a story.

Flight is a story.
Let there be light is a story.

Kate Gale

Tall Poppy

She walks around with her head in air.
Like she's somebody.

Who is she?
She came to town, built a library.

Who cares?
Who needs a library?

We have our own books.
We have our own parties.

She's never invited me to one of her parties.
Well, she invited me once.

Once I got there, she never talked to me.
Never offered me a glass of wine.

I do not understand it. Her brain must be
a crowded little place telling her, You're terrific!

She's fallen flat on her face now.
She'll be down for a while.

I used to think I could help her. I wanted to sit her down
say, slow down. Do what I say. You'll be okay.

I wanted to say, Keep your head down.
In this town, they'll eat you alive.

But she kept laughing and marching around
like she knew everything.

Now that she's flat on her face,
I hope she learns her lesson.

I hope she learns to keep her mouth shut.
She thought she was the tall poppy around here.

People like her get their houses burned down.
They get stung by a buzz of bees.

Their heads are cut off.
Goodbye tall poppy.

Kate Gale

Hazel Clayton Harrison

ODE FOR THE ROOTS OF ALTADENA

History books tells us it was the
Woodbury brothers, Fred and John

who purchased the lands
on which Altadena now stands

But if we dig deeper into the city's soil
we'll discover it was the blood, sweat, and toil

of many hands that labored to enrich the roots
of a land that produces such bountiful fruits

Long before Spanish soldiers landed on West Coast sands
Indian nations had for centuries inhabited these lands

In California they were known as Tongva
Those who dwelled in Altadena's hills and canyons
were known as the Haramokgna

Peacefully, they lived among bobcats and bears
cougars and coyotes

But what gifts did they leave to enrich today's economy?
To feed their families, Haramokgna men hunted and fished

They were often seen sailing downstream
their ti'ats overflowing with furs, fowls, and fishes

Their women taught us how to make breads
from wild oats and acorns
And oh, by chopping off prickly pear thorns
the sweet juices they made
more refreshing than ice cold lemonade

Yucca flower stalks, they steamed like asparagus and
from their fibrous leaves fishnets, shelters, and
baskets were weaved

Though the Haramokgna fought hard their culture to sustain
they soon lost battles to explorers from Spain
Yet, today their legacy remains

While emigrants from Mexico and Spain
came to stake their claim

Surviving Haramokgnas were driven into missions
to learn to speak English and be converted to Christians

As Hispanics grew prosperous, wealthy
caballeros and rancheros they became

Stretching far and wide over Altadena's hillsides
their ranches and adobes were a great source of pride

They brought with them Latin music and dancing and
throughout Altadena's lands played mariachi bands

Now let us pay tribute to the common man who
labored for the rich as cooks, care takers, and ranch hands

History books say that in Virginia John Brown
led the Harper's Ferry raid to liberate Blacks who'd
been enslaved

For his deeds, John Brown was captured and hanged
But he inspired Union armies that marched and sang

John Brown's body lies a moldin' in the grave
But his soul goes marching on
The stars above are looking kindly down
On the body of old John Brown

But few know that Brown's son Owen took part in that raid
He escaped to the West, and in the hills of Altadena

in a cabin with his brother Jason, Owen stayed
For joining the raid, Owen was never placed under arrest

Years later he passed away and above Altadena
on *Little Round Top* his body now rests

Perhaps Owen Brown's greatest legacy is to remind
us that all Americans have a right to be free!

All Americans have a right to be free!

Now let's honor the memory of a former slave
from Texas, Robert Owen was his name
He earned a living in El Prieto Canyon chopping wood
And made a small fortune investing in land

To help his less fortunate brethren he did all he could
He befriended a bondwoman named Bridget (Biddy) Mason
who'd been freed by California law

When her master tried to kidnap and re-enslave her
he sent his *vaqueros* to save her

In the late eighteen hundreds wealthy whites
migrated from the East and helped to build
Altadena's industry

On their Eaton Canyon ranch, the Bells, William and Emily
planted vineyards and built a winery

The Woodbury brothers not only planted deodar
cedars that still grace Christmas Tree Lane

But they sold their water rights to the Rubio Canon
Land and Water Association, and to this day
our water is supplied by that organization

In 1902 Altadena's first commercial building
The La Mariposa Hotel and Tavern was erected
on Lake Avenue

Run by the Webster family that building soon grew
into a shopping center that housed the Model Grocery store

And there in the nineteen twenties the U.S. Post Office
opened their doors

Today, we stand on hallowed ground cultivated
by many hands Red, White, Black, and Brown

Let us honor all those who helped our economy grow
strong and well

Our ancestors are buried here and among us
their spirits dwell

Like a mighty live oak Altadena's roots are many
Let us live together in peace, love, and harmony

Hazel Clayton Harrison

What Will We Do Today?

(For the Honorable Congressman and Civil Rights Leader John Lewis)
With courage, dignity, humility
We will rise with the morning sun
We will carry the torch you carried
Until victory has been won

We'll remember that bloody Sunday
Troopers you faced on Edmund Pettus Bridge
Billy clubs that fractured your skull
Yet you still fought to free us all from bondage

What will we do today?
We will rise with the morning sun
We will make 'good trouble'
and a way out of none

We will march through the hills of Georgia
Alabama, Mississippi, Tennessee
Through the valleys of Kentucky
Down winding roads to Washington D.C.

We will fight for rights paid for by
our ancestors with blood and tears
With courage and dignity, we will stand
through the long suffering years

What will we do today?
We will rise with the morning sun
To fight for the soul of our nation
Until a new day has begun.

Hazel Clayton Harrison

GEORGE FLOYD

When Derek Chauvin
pressed his knee
into your neck
he didn't know
who you were
He thought you were
a loser, a drug abuser, and
nobody would care
about another n*****
being murdered
in broad daylight
by a white cop
Oh, my Lord, he didn't
know you were a gentle
giant, a father, a brother
a Black mother's son
Didn't know that
when she heard your cry
she would rise from her grave
to wrap you in her arms
Didn't know the
Earth would quake
stars would refuse to shine
and people from
all over the world
would run into the streets
protesting and shouting
your name.

Hazel Clayton Harrison

IN THIS TIME OF PLAGUE

In this time of scorched earth
tinder of dried bones
red woods burning
dust swirling on
apocalyptic landscapes
In this time of corpses
piled up in trailers
like soldiers on
a battlefield
incinerators burning
day and night
air choked with the
stench of a holocaust
In this time of idle hands
too much time spent
in a devil's workshop
evil on the loose
lies on flaming swords
sacred institutions crumbling
the Constitution, a dry log
burning on a wood stove
In this time of hate

anger simmering
beneath a thin veneer
of civility
When a new term
essential workers
has been coined
for underpaid teachers
nurses, store clerks
sacrificial lambs

dying on front lines
In this time of
sickness and death
all it would take is
one match
just one lit match
for it all to go up
in smoke.

Hazel Clayton Harrison

THE WHITE HOUSE IS FALLING

January 6, 2020

The White House is falling
The White House is falling

Proud boys, right wing extremists
Qanon believers are storming
the Capital

They are carrying ropes
weapons, flags, plastic ties

They are shouting 'Hang Pence'
'We want Nancy!'

They are smashing windows
climbing walls

They are wandering through
chambers and halls

They are rifling through papers
chasing security guards
searching for Pence and Pelosi

The White House is falling
The White House is falling

Congressmen and women
are hiding behind locked doors

Where is the National Guard?
Where are the police?
Where are the soldiers?

They are standing down
They are standing down

The White House is falling
The White House is falling

Who will save us from terrorism?
Who will save our Democracy?

Hazel Clayton Harrison

THIS ANNIHILATION

There is in this annihilation an opening
a wind whirling a ship out to sea

After the wedding the bride and groom return
home to tend the hearth and make bread

Somehow, the honey tastes sweeter
This dying and being reborn leaves me breathless

Drifting in a dreamless sleep, I feel the fire
on my beloved's lips

I am smoke drifting through an open door.

Hazel Clayton Harrison

Published in *When the Virus Came Calling* by Golden Foothills Press, 2020

Gerda Govine Ituarte

Bloom

Today ideas bloom
want poetry to make
a difference in a world

gripped by fear and not knowing
how can poets make a difference
how can they help us breathe

how can they give us moments
filled with words that cause us
to laugh think feel be

let each of us as poets create
words that feed our souls
free our minds, make us thankful
to be alive

what can we do to till the soil
what can we do to calm the wind
let each of us as poets create
hope to relish sun on our face

rain on our backs and trees flowers
animals who shine for us
show off their best by just being there

We are the words
We are the readers
We are the ones who walk in the rain
between raindrops

We are the ones who light up the dark
keep door of possibilities ajar
We are the ones who offer our
poems as a gift to the world

One word at a time

Gerda Govine Ituarte

Published in *When the Virus Came Calling* by Golden Foothills Press, 2020

Becoming

Tension rips us apart
Caution does push ups
      Decisions collide

Weeds tie hands
Minute by minute we
     Disappear   reappear   lost
        Claw way back

Solution motionless
Weeds separate us
          Horizon shrinks
      Ground trembles

Off balance
Weeds pierce our ears
        Division close ranks
        Cloak of possibilities touch

Permission sets up house
Windows doors fly open
       Bright yellow flowers sway
      Fragrance of us Sweet

Gerda Govine Ituarte

Published in Altadena Literary Review (online), 2021-2022, Altadena, CA.

Personal

Uncover collect family stories
hidden in corners under hearts

words quench tongues on fire
life opens wide

wrap arms around us
as memories bite

go underneath
release nuggets of sweetness

while balancing on high wire

Gerda Govine Ituarte

Mothers Who Carry Their Own Water

When there is no well land is parched
mouth dusty skin cracked
bloody fingers plant thorn less roses

Mothers who carry their own water
are viewed with discomfort
curtains of words fall

I don't know what to say time heals all
whispers trail behind like tails
a reminder of what could happen to them

Mothers who carry their own water
live through, in, under, around
the death of their children

How?

They never ask why
lean on winds of change
find warmth in cold places

Push through survival to thrive
move beyond black and white
traverse shades of gray

Refuse to stay stuck in grave
dig deep for well inside

Gerda Govine Ituarte

Published in *Alterations | Thread Light Through Eye of Storm*,
2015, La Casa del Tùnel Productions, Pasadena, CA.

UKRAINE

U   R   N

K   I   N

R   U   N   RUNRUNRUN

A   R   E

I   N

N   U   K   E

E   E   R   I   E

Gerda Govine Ituarte

CALL IT WHAT IT IS

NO MORE SLAVERY
 NO MORE BUYING SELLING
  NO MORE LYNCHINGS
   NO MORE STRANGE FRUIT
    NO MORE DROWNINGS
     NO MORE DECAPITATION
      NO MORE BURNED BODIES
       NO MORE MISSING
        NO MORE RAPE
         NO MORE FIRES
          NO   MORE
           BEATINGS
            NO MORE
             BOMBINGS

CALL IT WHAT IT IS

G E [N O] C I DE

```
              M
              U
              R
              D
G E [N O] C I DE
U             E
N             R
S
```

THE "OTHER"

WIPE OFF FACE OF EARTH
CHILDREN TARGET ON THEIR BACKS

NO PROTECTION
NO HELP
NO ACCOUNTABILITY
NO JUSTICE JUST IS

HOLD HOSTAGE
POWER PATRONAGE PROFITABILITY
PURSE STRINGS
EMBEDDED EMBOLDENED

GENOCIDE WOVEN INTO FABRIC OF
AMERICA

OFFER PRAYERS CONDOLENCES
DOES NOT STOP GUN SALES

DOES NOT STOP BULLETS

DOES NOT STOP MASSACRES

DOES NOT STOP FILLIBUSTER

DOES NOT STOP POLITICAL IMPOTENCE

G
E
[N]
[O]
C
I
D
E

Gerda Govine Ituarte

Shahé Mankerian

American Baptism

As an American, Mother sees the ocean
for the first time in October. In Beirut,

she used the brook behind her house
to wash dishes because a misguided bomb

had ripped the copper pipes underneath
the sidewalks. Today, she stands on a pier,

stares at the faded blue of Santa Monica,
and remembers bloated bodies floating

on the Mediterranean. Her legs quiver
as she climbs down a rickety ladder and dips

her left foot into the water. The hesitant
sunset washes her skin with hues of lilac.

Her son calls her back on deck. In America,
only fools trust the oil-stained coastline.

In America, everyone drives a Cadillac.

Shahé Mankerian

Published in Border Crossing, volume 7, 2017

Blue Yarn

Here, your eldest clears cobwebs
behind the upright piano and finds

the blue sweater button you lost
before the burial. You're not there

to claim it. Turn the page: Here,
your middle child under a mulberry

tree unravels your blue sweater
with moth holes on the sleeve

and coffee stains on the insignia.
Turn the page: In the backyard,

your youngest son finds the blue,
tangled yarn and rolls the skein

into a ball. He lights a cigarette
and starts knitting a winter cap

for his daughter. In the epilogue,
he adds a frail, blue pompon

to resemble a rabbit's tail.

Shahé Mankerian

Published in FU Review Issue 9, 2020

I Didn't Want Mama to Kiss Me Anymore

Every morning, she drove me to school
in Father's Chevrolet. The radio spewed static.

She parked crooked by the curb and allowed
the engine to idle so it won't die. The heavy

metal clique against the no parking wall
smoked cigarettes. Mama with her maroon

lipstick reached over and kissed me
underneath the twisted sycamore. I rubbed

my face and prayed Sylvia, the girl I loved
since seventh grade, never saw this. Once,

during English period, Mrs. Reyna, read
my poem to the class: When you turn

seventeen, cram Mama in a box, duct tape
the lids quickly, so she'll never come out.

Shahé Mankerian

Published in Silver Birch Press, January 2017

Mama, Beirut Burns Tonight

The smoke blossoms like mushroom
and caresses against the stratosphere,

your giant TV, where you keep seeing
the same men, with cigars and semen-

stained suits, soil on their soles, ash
imprints, snickering, as they squeeze

their vermin-infested bellies through
the backdoor of the national bank,

where they stash dollars like heaps
of piling trash, pillaging into the night.

Mama, you don't have to watch.
You've seen this episode before:

the unwilling sunrise after a contorted
nightmare, the lingering pink haze,

a tender bird too broken to fly, the music
whimpers as the credits become a blur.

Shahé Mankerian

Published in FU Review, June 9, 2020

Third Dream

You wore the salmon-colored dress
with matching shoes. The scales
on your pantyhose sparkled

against the smoked, paprika sun.
Don't be alarmed, you said.
This is the third dream

I interrupted tonight. I wanted
to sit up, rub the sleep crust
from my eyes, drag myself

into the kitchen, and fix you
the cardamom coffee you loved.
But I stayed, gripping the comforter,

or was it the hem of your dress?
I didn't want to blur your towering
silhouette or overexpose the celluloid

of this dream. A mother walks
into the bedroom of her sleeping son.
Cut. Wearing a salmon-colored dress.

Shahé Mankerian

Published in Coastal Shelf, 2020

In Twos

My mother toys with dementia.
Our conversations volley between

poetry and my failure to produce
another child. She recites verses

from ancient Armenia because
she remembers them from school.

I feed her memory pills
as she mutters, "Two cranes falter

from our world…" She chews
on air as if to adjust her dentures.

"Your daughter looks lonely like
a lost sandal," she reminds me

and holds my hand in her kitchen
because I'm her second born,

because we don't have much
to say, because silence provides

another poem. "My son, find
the missing pair, the other

goddess, the carnival of joy…"

Shahé Mankerian

Published Sun Journal, December 2018, Dyad Issue

Toni Mosley

Sunday Dinners

I do a Soul Train glide over

To the pantry for oil and spices

Then a cha-cha to the cupboard

Of pots and pans

A hully gully to the fridge for meats

And vegetables

I do a slip of the hip which I sprinkle

Taste on what I'm cookin and when

It's done it's hot and tasty with

Loud music and hot spices.

Toni Mosley

MAYA ANGELOU

TONI MORRISON

GWENDOLYN BROOKS

Sistahs all
Black, Beautiful, and Smart

Some Nobel winners
Some Pulitzers

Who worked through many dawns
To lay the groundwork

For me to walk upon

Toni Mosley

Alabama Bound on the Jim Crow Line

Grandma often told
the story
of taking my mother,
her daughter
and my mother's brothers,
grandma's sons
to
Mobile, Alabama
in summer
riding white
First class
travelling to the mouth
of the South
Mobile, Alabama
on the Jim Crow Line.

At summer's end
with sunburned skin
Mama and her brothers
no longer white
all rode black
going back
the train holding course
travelling North
on the Jim Crow Line.

Toni Mosley

Published in Pasadena Rose Poets Poetry Collection 2019

Inherited Legacies

Here is what I inherited from my family:
The love of alcohol. Daddy loved Jack Daniels. Scotch, water
back. At night.
Mama loved Smirnoff Vodka and orange juice. Morning, noon, and night.
I love wine. No special brand. Whatever's on hand. Mama and her four
brothers were heavy drinkers. My husband complains I'm not far behind.

Then there's the threat of disease---
Cancer – the Big C
Daddy's daddy had it
Daddy's sister had it
Daddy's brother had it
Mama's mama had it
My sister had it
I had it and am the lone survivor I'm proud to say.

Then there's the Sugar—as diabetes was called back in the day.
Mama's brother lost a foot then a leg then his mind.

We had no church. No religion. Daddy had quarrels with religion. Mama
had quarrels with Daddy about religion. I married a man with quarrels
around religion. Mama's Mama had no quarrels with religion. She was
Pentecostal. That scared me. So I've had quarrels with religion. No family
church, no family bible, and never learned to pray.

And…Then there was trauma.

Daddy's brother killed his wife then himself. Left two babies crying.
Daddy killed himself. The black news said he was despondent. The white
news said nothing. Back then blacks were no news.
My uncle's son was shot and killed as he slept.

1960 was the year I just wept and wept.

Toni Mosley

Published in Altadena Poetry Anthology 2019

Oooh Baby Baby

If songwriters wrote songs
Without
Oooh baby baby

And
Poets wrote rhyme
Without
Oooh baby baby

And
Artists made art
Without
Oooh baby baby

Where would love be
Without
Oooh baby baby?

Toni Mosley

Published in Pasadena Rose Poets Poetry Collection 2019

A Room of My Own

After reading Virginia Woolf's book, *A Room of One's Own,* I became enthralled with creating my own space. She wrote, "women must have money and privacy in order to write." Woolf's focus was on women with literary genius, not the ordinary woman who lacked money and competence. She also wrote, "money cannot be earned; it must come to the writer in the form of a windfall or a legacy or it will bring with it attachment, obligations."

Years ago, I came into a six-figure windfall that allowed me to convert a third bedroom into a space of my own. It was used as a storage room. I could now clean it out and make space for me to read, write, and create. At the time I didn't know how or what to write until I started attending writing workshops and began to recall childhood memories. A facilitator at one of those workshops told me that she thought I had writing talent and introduced me to her agent. That's when writing memoir began to take hold and having a room of my own became important.

I phoned the Salvation Army to make arrangements for them to haul away the stained gray camelback sofa, the old desk, and chairs. The floor was covered with stacks of books that needed organizing. I headed to Ikea in Burbank in search of a new sofa and a bookcase. Finding a sofa was an unsuccessful journey, but happily I found the perfect bookcase, paid $250, and scheduled an appointment for delivery and installation. Within two days Ikea was at my door. The delivery men unpacked it, screwed it to the floor and wall for earthquake safety, and I could see change beginning to take place. The stacks of book that covered the floor now had a home.

The search for a new sofa continued. I found a short white sofa with two huge pillows on display in the window of a small European furniture boutique in Pasadena, paid $600 for it, and arranged for next day delivery. Excitement was taking hold with this conversion project of creating a room of my own.

Next, I found a desk with an adjustable chair on sale at Staples in Monrovia and paid $120 for the set. My husband and I loaded them onto his truck for free transport home. Now I needed to get rid of the dusty old window blinds. Realizing that Calico Corners fabric store was nearby in Arcadia, I headed over and found the perfect Bohemian fabric for curtains and coordinating pillow covers. I quickly paid the cost for my order, came home, and decided to have my windows and carpet professionally cleaned for $200.

Within days of the window washing and carpet cleaning, Ed, from Calico Corners showed up with my new curtains draped over his right arm and rods in his left hand. I was thrilled. This was the last and most expensive touch $800 for the room of my own.

It felt good not having to ask my husband for his approval or his money. I meant no second opinions, no arguments, no attachments, no obligations.

As my room began to take hold, I no longer saw myself as ordinary and incompetent. I began to dream of becoming the literary genius in Woolf's book.

Toni Mosley

Published in Altadena Literary Review 2020

Carla Sameth

Love Letter to a Burning World

Southern California 2020

Praise the dark that covers us with ashes,
this morning's tears, reminding us why we cherish
the not-burning baby cry of awake, not heartbreak.

Mom, I need a hug, please,
I just can't seem to do anything right.
Raphael, the angel name, should we have birthed
a warrior instead, one who could fight the demons?

I can't say for sure I'm an addict but I'm doing too much.
He gets up, then decides he'd rather smoke,
not feeling OK right now.
I am twisted up, feel the same way. Not OK.

No, son, what you are feeling are singed embers
after six months of shutdown. Broken glass.
Murder after murder of men and women the color of your skin.
At traffic stops, in the dark, in bed, while jogging. Anywhere.

Praise the path that brought you here today, a boomerang.
Mom, I can't make it, I'm at the car repair, I need
to keep looking for someone who can fix this.
The drop like we hear in music, I hear it in his soul.

My face is wet as he leaves in a gust:
I have to meet my friends at the demonstration, I'll feel better.
More purpose. Do you kill a child by holding or letting go?
Ashes, ashes as he runs out the door.

Doesn't he know this is an emergency?
Like the blare of fire warning,
Pack your bags comes from the evacuation order.

Today his voice searing into my chest.
Praise his tears for crying with me.
Praise the seat that holds me fast.

Carla Sameth

Published in Call Me Literary Journal, University of Alabama 2021

June 2020: Alarm goes off,

I clutch my wife, remember
to breathe, remember
George Floyd, remember
Christopher Ballew
21, assaulted by police
up the street, in Altadena,
remember the names,
the deaths. Nonstop.
Fear floods in, room congested.
A poet wrote me a poem
that says think of your son
when you first wake up
and I do—but terror for
the risk to his soul,
his body, his skin.
This mom's heart
tumbles, even with
my wife opening the curtain,
singing me *good morning,*
good morning, even with
wild parrots and cascading
Pasadena birdsong,
the cat kneading and purring.
Even then, I cannot calm
when my wife gets up to leave.
I see three missed calls last night—
probably just son telling me
about the latest protest.

He made me laugh
at the Highland Park march—
Mom, look. That white woman.

Full Black Panther regalia,
knee high black boots,
black coveralls and beret,
fist raised, standing in front
of that MLK mural on the wall
of that hipster coffee shop?
(Would it be her Instagram post?)
The woman, she looked at me, just said,
Your life matters.

Yes, it does, son,
and I imagine
telling him this every day,
what I've always
told him:
his life means.
But the words sink into fear,
get stuck in the throat,
legs still glued to the bed,
mind gripped by galloping thoughts.
I pull the blanket over my head.

Carla Sameth

Published in What is Left 2021

The Fragility of Home

Mom, I don't think I should see you this week.
Best friend's roommate's boyfriend's roommate—their bubble—has Covid.
When did my son float in and out of my bubble?

*

Used to be I'd introduce the music to my son. His dad and I listened to,
'70s soul and funk. I took him to see Al Green, Stevie Wonder, Earth
Wind and Fire.
In kindergarten, he played in little boy band "The Blasters" with Janice
Marie Vercher
(Taste of Honey). Now he sends me a Spotify list 30 hours 19 minutes
for my wife and I to dance out pandemic blues—

House Music for the Soul, my way of describing what house music means to me.

Whirl bodies about, shoulders sway, legs move forward and back, lifting
and kicking, butt shaking. Dancing, lips turned to laughter, I think
of my son.
Our tiny, cluttered living room. Pushing back the mosaic kidney-shaped
coffee table.

One day I found him listening to Joni Mitchell. *This guy.* Dreamy
intellectual,
And I once danced to "Ojos negros, piel canela" baby in sling.
Crinkly eyes, old café au lait face. Fireworks temperament.
Soft blankie touch. Out of eight pregnancies, he was the only one
who lived.

    One live birth.

*

At home I hear, *I love you so, so much, Mom.* Home is where I see my baby become a young man. A young Black man. And fear is what violates that home.
Murder happens live: George Floyd, Ahmaud Arbery, Breonna Taylor.
A running catalogue of voices.

We talk about:

>   Kendrick Lamar – *Alright*
>   Leon Bridges – *Sweeter*
>   Anderson Paak – *Lockdown*
>   Harold Melvin and the Blue Notes — *Wake up*
>   Old school Gil Scott-Heron

*

I live in the house I bought when my son was young, the only house I've owned. What does home smell like? Garlic, soy sauce, vinegar, bay leaf, ginger, chile, Chinese five spice.
What I learned amidst Tagalog and Ilokano in South Seattle became food for my son in LA.

I roam the Pasadena neighborhood. Wild grass comforts even with its scent like piss. Mint floats in iced tea, sage brushes nose, lavender cools battered soul, basil blesses our meal. Turquoise, Provence blue, red, gold and orange, bright bold bougainvillea colors paint our little Pasadena cottage Caribbean.

*

In the Early Years, baby boy sweat melted onto me, while I pushed stroller, pass Roscoe's Chicken and Waffles, pass Popeyes, pass Pollo Unico—the Chinese-Peruvian restaurant. We ordered 20 chickens to eat in nearby McDonald Park for his second birthday.

Let them see you, get to know you, my mom instructed. *Walk the neighborhood.*

Alien helicopters buzzed overhead, under siege, signal constant threat,
not-yet-groomed bathrobe-clad woman wandered muttering
They shoot people and jump into our backyards. I was a single mother
hoped the house would be home, looking for safety.
This home grew us, and then we left.

Ten Years Later, I come back ashamed that starter home became
my finisher home. Now home is where I sit on patio, curse
between teeth, too many months of quarantine, where I teach
summer writing camp to teenagers on Zoom, where my wife and I breathe
in our shared space. That is what spells love.

And yet home is where loneliness crawls into my bones, stealthy
as any virus. I can't bear the compressed space anymore: some days
take to the jasmine-flecked hills, past the bags of giveaway lemons,
steep stairways of Silverlake and Echo Park, where my 24-year-old son
now lives for socially distanced visits, masked.

For Mother's Day he buys me lavender iced latte and a dulce de
leche muffin
oozing sweet caramel into my waiting lips.
We share muffins— but later I think of red spikes and being irresponsible.

*

Home still means birds we can't name, birds who serenade us;
we recognize the mourning doves, the wild parrots, the hummingbirds.
Others fill our ears a shared symphony. My son pops in on FaceTime.
Asks, *How are you, Mom?*

He turns my question back on me when I ask,
Have you had a lot of ups and downs?

> *I have.* Home is the son and wife I know
> will softly touch my wilting heart when most needed
> and least expected.

Carla Sameth

Published in What is Left 2021

The Gods in the Middle of Election Week

The god of my ears listens to my son's playlists. A pandemic playlist made to keep us moving when all appeared frozen, including the arms that reached out for a hug, the lips for a kiss, the hands to touch. The election week playlist to get us through this week when I figure out what was true for so many years already, that I can't always tell him, *Everything will be ok,* but the god of his soul includes songs like, "Pray Momma Don't Cry" by Rapsody, "The Times They Are A-Changin'" by Bob Dylan, "Fight the Power" by Public Enemy and "Lockdown" with Anderson .Paak. Oh and "I Can't Breathe" by H.E.R. He tells me that he does believe he'll be OK, even went roller skating with his friends, found a pathway to the god of his heart, moving joyed-up limbs to his skating playlist, even though he says, *I am so tired of people not getting it.*

*

The god of my motherhood was with me when my son was hooked up to machines and how his heart didn't stop after swallowing 80-100 Robitussin caplets. Those times. The god of my belly remembers him floating there for nine months when all the others died long before they could become my living child. A faint scar plus this grown living one reminds me of this god, as he tells me, *Mom I'll take you to the doctor for your appointment; I'm not afraid of needles.*

*

It is possible that the god of my eyes was with me when they found out my eye was swollen, the arteries blocked, the blood pooling from what they told me was an eye stroke, too much stress, a wake-up call. The god of trumpet playing stepped in to bring this to my attention; I started playing after a 40+ year pause, and the notes were becoming more and more blurry which sent me to the optometrist, the ophthalmologist, the retina specialist who showed me the pools of blood, the blocked artery, and the swollen retina and told me about the injections I would get every 4-6 weeks, way too many times. But the god of all sweetness was there and so was my wife and son who watched the needles go in.

*

And I know the god of the shattered heart showed up too, to remind me that even if I want to say this election, all these people—whose god is white supremacy—show us that everything will *not* be ok, my son is still skating *whoosh, slide, jump, turn*, headphones on, believing in the god of hope, salty ocean breeze touching his cheek, as he wheels around and around, body moving to music, waves lapping that long shore.

Carla Sameth

I am a woman of almost 62 years old,

of no special bravery.
Every day, I wake up to my wife
clutching me tightly, then singing loudly,
and the cat, once a teen mama, pounding on the door,
last night's gunshots not yet forgotten.
Turn up the sound I say,
that song about waking up and working hard each day
though I am a woman inert, until I decide
to throw off all the weighted memories—
falling down interiors, the magic elastic
that holds my unkind body
tight to my imagination,
until I step out and blow kisses
to the hummingbird, frantic, ecstatic,
or just doing its job,
circling the Bird of Paradise.

Two years older than I was when
my son, friends, and family threw
that party for me,
the trio playing songs I'd once danced to,
baby in sling, like "Piel Canela,"
the *carne*, the *aguas, las flores,*
pastel de las tres leches.
My friend Gary showed up
only to jump from a parking structure weeks later.
He'd told me, *It's been a rough year*
and I agreed, *it's been a year*
and he said, *we'll talk.*
But we never did, not really.
He only called me to tell me how proud
he was of me, my son, all we've done.
And damn him, he didn't wait for that conversation

about the obliterating fog, the deep downward slide,
the gray gray as if he were another Seattle child,
or whatever said to him,
Jump Gary, jump.

I am a woman almost 62
who once had moxie, chopped wood,
built trails, leaped in front of skinheads
who threatened me and my two sisters.

A tiny speck lost in a corner
wondering if I'll rise up and blow out to the sky
when we finally can open the doors.
62, but still the nail
that may not bend,
the mango sweet and spicy,
chile and limon that bring a mouth alive.
The lips that remember the softest kisses
billowing across continents
only to discover they were once here,
right beside me.
The skater leaping,
flying, shimmying a fountain
of joy and since I'm not gliding,
my son is. Sliding through Venice Beach
and home again to me.
I am the arms that held him,
milky sweet sweat, then opened up skyward
to the honeyed moon and the bright, bright stars.

Carla Sameth

Published in We Were Not Alone Anthology 2021

Your Eyes are Seacolor but Do You Remember?

The walls of that grotto
were everycolor blue
and you said, "Look! Your eyes are seacolor.

Anne Sexton "The Nude Swim"

Your eyes are thirsty capsules

    as if onyx could be blue, smooth amalgam.

Our rifts cannot last long, the ubiquitous

    You don't listen, you're shutdown

        You're too emotional, too loud, calm down.

I feel these days as if I trespass

    your territory so unknown—do you see me

as vapid, wishing only to manifest the breasts now gone?

    I look to the sky, the clearest blue, street white snow-spotted.

    If I could knit, I would answer my questions by making you a cap.

Instead, I write this poem, think of crisp green apples and the time I saw you

    standing in California Plaza. "Too young" I thought, but cute, very pretty.

I used to love to hold you, one breast cupped in my hand. Now I hold you

    arms careful not to touch that place of removed flesh.

Is it enough to say *I love you, I'd never leave you?*

Am I a killjoy if I complain of missing you as woman? Tough, mannish,

but sometimes you cried like a broken ragdoll. Now you brush me

and my tears away, as if I am a mosquito or pesky fly.

Carla Sameth

Annette Wong

CALLIGRAPHY

When I learned to write,
my mother began with the elements:

Earth   土
and fire   火
water   水
and wood 木.

Then,
the sky   天,
its sun   日
and moon 月,
clouds   云,
and rain   雨.

Brush to black ink, our hands
traversing the smooth page.

My mother's voice,
her guiding hand

painting the world
in bold strokes.

Annette Wong

Published in Altadena Poetry Review 2017

NOONDAY DEMON

Before you prepare your pyre
and set yourself ablaze

before you start your running jump
or walk calmly towards the water

before you draw the curtains
and put yourself to sleep

try, if you can,
to withstand

even a moment
longer.

Annette Wong

Published in Pasadena Rose Poets Poetry Collection 2019

DRAMA

David Mamet says

*there is no such thing
as character.*

Only things people do
and say.

Drama is plot. Everything
in service of story.

All utterances: myths.
Lies.

If an incident fails to further
the story, cut it out.

Like a joke,
all good

drama tends towards
the punch

line.

Annette Wong

Published in Altadena Poetry Review 2018

Interstitial

Always I am leaping.

A gazelle, stotting,
back arched
head down.

Say *crossing*
Say *consciousness*.

M. tells me I am hard to know,
I am unreliable
as shape shifters are prone.

Call it *adaptation*.

How I've mastered it—
the way I move between worlds. Seamless
but still – there are stitches.

See how thread treads fiber
how it must vanish
to reappear.

Let me train your gaze.
Adjust the aperture. See the gazelle
in the crosshairs

how she appears
to fly, all fours lifting
from the ground?

Annette Wong

Published in Lantern Review 2019

TUOL SLENG*

When the power went,
there had been rain for five days,
scattering the hawkers, the *motos*,
the men sprawled in their *tuktuks*.
Ants flecked the rambutan plucked
from a wet market stall,
days shy of ripe.

I live behind the Genocide Museum. I wrote home.
It sounds grimmer than it is.

It wasn't the spattered tiles
that got to me most,
or the whites of eyes captured
on camera, the metal beds
on which bodies were strung—but the thought—
of each prisoner's last glimpse
of sun, ruptured, through the shutters
and perforated walls
before the blindfolds, the transport,
fifteen kilometers to *Choeung Ek*,
the Killing Fields, where speakers hung
from The Magic Tree** blaring:

Children, do not forget the fresh blood of our soldiers and
Children, forever remember the revolution!

Now, darkness. New sounds audible,
without the percussive rain and hum of motors:
ceramic on tin, the neighbors' dinner utensils
set to rest. In the alley, children
with candles, laughing. The patter

of hands on smooth surfaces, the collective search
for something to light.

* Tuol Sleng, also known as Security Prison (S-21), was a former high school in Phnom Penh, Cambodia, which the Khmer Rouge turned into an execution center. Prisoners who were not killed at S-21 were transported to the Killing Fields for execution. It is now a Genocide Museum.
** The Magic Tree is a tree in the *Choeung Ek* killing fields upon which the Khmer Rouge strung loudspeakers that played propaganda and music as victims were being executed.

Annette Wong

Published in Altadena Poetry Review 2017

PASADENA ROSE POETS BIO

Teresa Mei Chuc was born in Sài Gòn, Việt Nam and immigrated to the U.S. as a refugee with her mother and brother shortly after the Việt Nam War while her father, who had served in the Army of the Republic of Việt Nam, remained in a Viet Cong "reeducation" prison camp for nine years. Poet Laureate Emerita of Altadena, California (Editor-in-Chief) 2018-2020 and a member of the Pasadena Rose Poets, Teresa Mei Chuc is the author of three collections of poetry, *Red Thread* (Fithian Press, 2012 & republished by Shabda Press, 2021), *Keeper of the Winds* (FootHills Publishing, 2014), and *Invisible Light* (Many Voices Press, 2018). Teresa and Doug Rawlings, American veteran of the Việt Nam War, published a collaborative poetry book, *Cầu Tre / Bamboo Bridge: Conversations between a Vietnamese Boat Refugee and an American Veteran of the Việt Nam War – Told in Poetry and Prose* (Kellscraft Studio, November 2021).

Damian is a Bronx born, Los Angeles cultivated artist, writer, and filmmaker. Born Damian Gonzalez, he signs his work without his surname. Damian has worked in the film industry since 2014 at studios like NBC Universal, Bad Robot, and Netflix. His poetry first appeared in the 2017 *Altadena Poetry Review Anthology* and was included in the *Pasadena Rose Poets Poetry Collection 2019*. In late 2021/early 2022, he combined his love of poetry with his passion for visual storytelling and co-directed *An Inertial Frame of Reference*, a short film trilogy of his published works. His visual poetry films have played online and at festivals including Film Crash, Northwest Film Forum's Cadence Video Poetry Fest, Pan Eros FF, Ottawa Kino, and the Oregon Short Film Festival. He's honored to be included in this new collection amongst brilliantly talented writers, and proud to be given the opportunity to call himself a Pasadena Rose Poet.

Dr. Kate Gale is Co-founder and Managing Editor of Red Hen Press, and Editor of the Los Angeles Review. She teaches in the Low Residency MFA program at the University of Nebraska in Poetry, Fiction and Creative Non-Fiction. She is the author of *The Loneliest Girl* from the University of New Mexico Press and of seven books of poetry including *The Goldilocks Zone* from the University of New Mexico Press in 2014, *Echo Light* from Red Mountain in 2014, and six librettos including *Rio de Sangre*, a libretto for an opera with composer Don Davis, which had its world premiere October 2010 at the Florentine Opera in Milwaukee. She speaks on independent publishing at schools including USC, Harvard, Columbia, and Oxford University. Her opera in process is https://www.thewebopera.com/ and an opera on Che Guevara is in process with Cuban composer Armando Bayolo. Her opera on Esther written for the singer Hila Plitmann is in process with the composer Mark Abel.

Hazel Clayton Harrison is a Pushcart Prize nominee. She served as Altadena Poet Laureate/Community Events from 2018-2020. Working closely with her co-Poet Laureate/Editor in Chief, she helped to edit the *Altadena Poetry Review 2019* and *Altadena Literary Review 2020*. Her book, *Down Freedom Road*, was published in 2020 by Shabda Press. Her poetry has been widely published in literary journals such as the *Altadena Literary Review* 2020, *Coiled Serpent*, *Grandfathers*, *A Rock Against the Wind*, *River Crossings,* and *When the Virus Came Calling.* She is the author of a children's book, *The Story of Christmas Tree Lane,* and a memoir, *Crossing the River Ohio.* She is a co-owner and operator of Jah Light Media, an editing and publishing consulting firm. As a member of the Pasadena Rose Poets ensemble, she enjoys reciting poetry at venues throughout Southern California.

Dr. Gerda Govine Ituarte established the Pasadena Rose Poets in 2016, created lunch-time readings 2016 & 2018, and poetry readings at Pasadena City Council Meetings, 2017-2019. She is Editor of the Pasadena Rose Poets' first *Poetry Collection, 2019, Reflection. Resistance. Reckoning. Resurrection.* and the second, *Pasadena Rose Poets Poetry Collection, 2022, Not So Perfect Storm*. Govine Ituarte is the author of four books, *Poetry Within Reach in Unexpected Places,* 2018; *Future Awakes* in Mouth of NOW 2016; *Alterations | Thread Light Through Eye of Storm* 2015; and *Oh, Where is My Candle Hat?* 2012. Govine Ituarte received a Certificate of Recognition, from Supervisor Joel Anderson, Second District, San Diego County *In special recognition of your contribution in celebrating the legacy of poetry in the community and for being a champion of our region's rich literary heritage.* She was accepted into the Carrizozo Artist Residency February 2022. Her poetry is included in *Scenes of Southern California: A Directory of So. Cal Poets 2022, Gathering A Women Who Submit Anthology 2021, Altadena Poetry Review 2021*, and *When the Virus Came Calling 2020.* Govine Ituarte received her doctorate from Teachers College Columbia University.

 **Shahé Mankerian** is the principal of St. Gregory Hovsepian School in Pasadena and the director of mentorship at the International Armenian Literary Alliance (IALA). He is the former Co-director of the Los Angeles Writing Project. He is the recipient of the Los Angeles Music Center's BRAVO Award, which recognizes teachers for innovation in arts education. In 2021, Mankerian's debut poetry collection, *History of Forgetfulness*, was published by Fly on the Wall Press in the UK. The collection was a semifinalist for the prestigious Khayrallah Prize and a finalist at the Bibby First Book Competition, the Crab Orchard Poetry Open Competition, the Quercus Review Press Poetry Book Award, and the White Pine Press Poetry Prize.

Toni Mosley has been writing since age 12. As a former nonprofit executive, she was responsible for telling stories about her organization and its constituents. She retired in 2013 to become a professional writer of confessional poetry and completed her memoir, *Dead Flies on the Window Sill*, a hybrid of poetry; prose and essays about growing up in a chaotic household. Her work has been featured in the Pasadena Rose Poets Poetry Collection 2019, Altadena Poetry Review Anthology 2019, Spectrum Magazine #23, 2020, and reading venues includes Walt Disney Concert Hall, Barnes & Noble Bookstore, Pasadena Central Library, and City of Pasadena Council Chambers.

Carla Rachel Sameth was recently selected as the Co-Poet Laureate for Altadena, CA 2022-2024. Her chapbook, *What Is Left* was published December 2021 with Dancing Girl Press. Carla's debut memoir, *One Day on the Gold Line,* originally published in 2019, will be reissued by Golden Foothills Press in 2022. Her writing on blended/unblended, queer, multi-racial and single parent families appears in a variety of literary journals, anthologies, newspapers, and blogs including: *The Rumpus, Full Grown People, MUTHA Magazine, Brain/Child, Brevity Blog, Entropy, Anti-Heroin Chic, Global Poemic, Soren Lit, La Bloga, Call Me {Progress} Literary Journal/University of Alabama* and *The Nervous Breakdown.* Carla's work has been twice named as Notable Essays of the Year in *Best American Essays.* Her story "Graduation Day at Addiction High," which originally appeared in *Narratively,* was also selected for *Longread's* "Five Stories on Addiction." A Pasadena Rose Poet, a West Hollywood Pride Poet, and a former PEN Teaching Artist, Carla teaches creative writing to high school and university students and taught incarcerated youth. She was selected as a Carrizozo Artist-in-Residence (February 2022). She lives in Pasadena with her beloved partner, Milo. https://carlasameth.com/

Annette Wong is currently enrolled in the MFA program for writers at Warren Wilson College. She studied History and International Studies at Yale and Law at the University of Southern California. Her work has been supported by the following fellowships, workshops, and opportunities: The Rona Jaffe Foundation Graduate Fellowship in Creative Writing, AWP (Association of Writers and Writing Programs) Writer to Writer Mentorship, Bread Loaf Writers' Conference, The Community of Writers, Palm Beach Poetry Festival, Writing Workshops Los Angeles, and Voices of Our Nations Arts Foundation (VONA). Her work appeared in Lantern Review 2019, Pasadena Rose Poets Poetry Collection 2019, and Waxwing Poetry Northwest 2019. She lives in Los Angeles with her husband and enjoys the journey as a first-time Mom.

****

Artist Luis Ituarte

As an artist, I like to disclose the creative process by all avenues available to me. The objects I create; paintings, collages, sculptures, poetry and writings, along with the activities I generate; art programs, art events, political art interventions, cultural celebrations, curatorial practice, art exhibits, and teaching, are all part of my expression of humanity. My work's real value is fulfilled when it interacts with people and brings out our cultural, social and individual personas for the common good; it is then that I'm an artist! Art lives in human culture and it is with my art that I try to explain who I am in that culture. My intent is to create by reviewing history, observing nature's ways and participating in the politics of culture as a process to invite transformation for the best possible future.
www.luisituarte.com

****

Photographer Alfred Haymond

Los Angeles Native and long-time Altadena resident, Alfred Haymond, continues to distinguish himself as an accomplished photographer. His images are consistently on display and part of installations throughout the San Gabriel Valley and greater Westside area. Lauded for both his collaboration and solo works in exhibits such as – "Black Men Shoot" (Alkebu-lan Cultural Center 2017), "Celebrating Diversity Through Photography" (Cook Art Gallery 2018), Pasadena's annual "Observations in Black" (Citywide since 2017), the film noir inspired, "Tales of Pasadena" (Jackie Robinson Center, Art Night 2019), and "Convergence @The Metaphor" (Metaphor Club, Los Angeles 2019). Alfred Haymond offers the viewer a glimpse of his seemingly vintage composition style and nostalgic approach to the medium. When asked about his ardent fascination with black & white photograph, Alfred readily explains; *"It's just where my head is at. It's thought provoking to the eye and therapeutic to the mind."*
www.ObservationalPhotograpy.com

Pasadena Rose Poets
Poetry Collection 2022
Not So Perfect Storm

Pasadena Rose Poets Tapestry

Third dream…The Unknown Woman…Tasting the Rain…Beyond the breakers…Expulsion from Eden…In twos…Snakes In My Hair…Blue Yarn…Wound Care…

THE WHITE HOUSE IS FALLING…IN THIS TIME OF PLAGUE…

THIS ANNIHILATION BECOMING PERSONAL…American Baptism…The Gods in the Middle of Election Week…Call it what it is…

Medusa's Cookbook…Sunday Dinner…Inherited Legacies I Didn't Want Mama to Kiss Me Anymore…Alarm goes off…The Fragility of Home… Noonday Demon…Drama…Crying Makes You Feel Better…What Will We Do Today…

GEORGE FLOYD…Mothers Who Carry Their Own Water… UKRAINE…The Dead & The Living…Your Eyes are Seacolor but Do you Remember?…

I am a woman of almost 62 years old…A Room of My Own…Oooh Baby…Personal…Tall Poppy…Wildfire…Love Letter to a Burning World Southern California 2020…Chinese Female Kung Fu Super Heroes… Nobels & Pulitzers…Today…Hanging…Calligraphy…In All the Movies… Warm Water…Bubble…Hands…Bloom…

Cover Art by Luis Ituarte

Photographs by Alfred Haymond

www.ingramcontent.com/pod-product-compliance
Lightning Source LLC
Chambersburg PA
CBHW032129090426
42743CB00007B/522